CARAVAGGIO COLORING BOOK

8 Masterpieces from the Master

ARTHUR BENJAMIN

"The world is but a canvas to our imagination."
—Henry David Thoreau

ABOUT THE ARTIST

Caravaggio is the name of the artist's native village, near Bergamo in Italy. A pupil of Simone Peterzano, he studied a lot on his own, so the development of his style is not entirely known. Caravaggio worked in Rome, Naples and Malta where he led a scandalous, extraordinary life. Although he was forgotten until 1920s, he always remained a revolutionary in his own time. He was the master of chiaroscuro and of dramatic effects. The power of nature and truth inspired him, so he painted everyday people in the manner of naturalism.

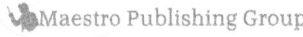Maestro Publishing Group

Pubished by Maestro Publishing Group

Printed in the United States of America
ISBN: 978-1619494862

CONTENTS

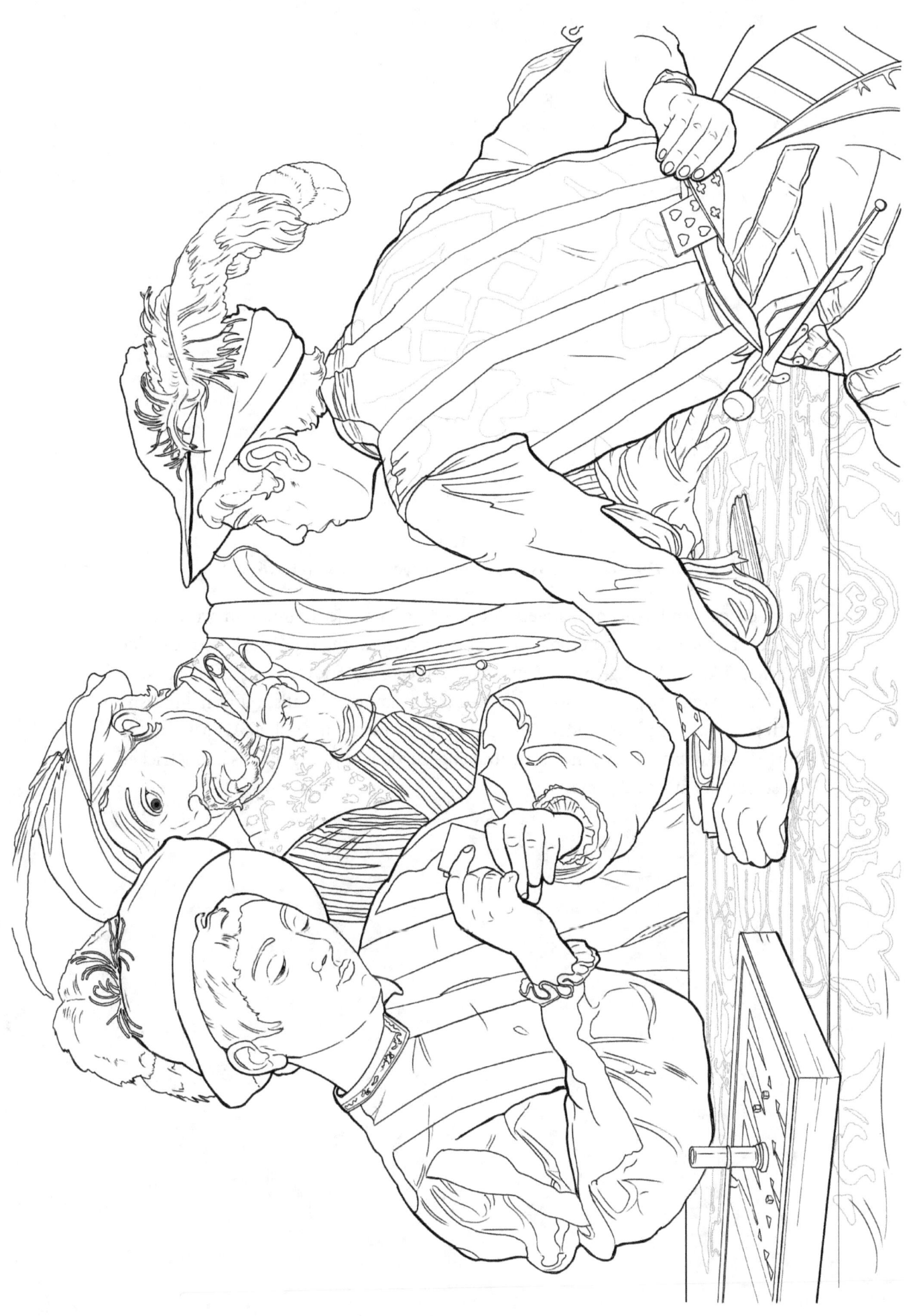

3

Plate 1.
The Cardsharps (The Cardplayers) c. 1594-1596

Dark corners and dangerous streets of Rome, the ambience of inns and brothels, the world of adventurers and crooks-it all inspired Caravaggio to break with the Old Masters, like Michelangelo and Raphael, and create an innovative style. He pursued truth and simplicity in art, so he painted in a manner of realism and naturalism, with common people as models. This painting, currently in Kimbell Art Museum in Fort Worth (Texas, USA), shows an amusing incident: a young man is being tricked by scammers in a card game.

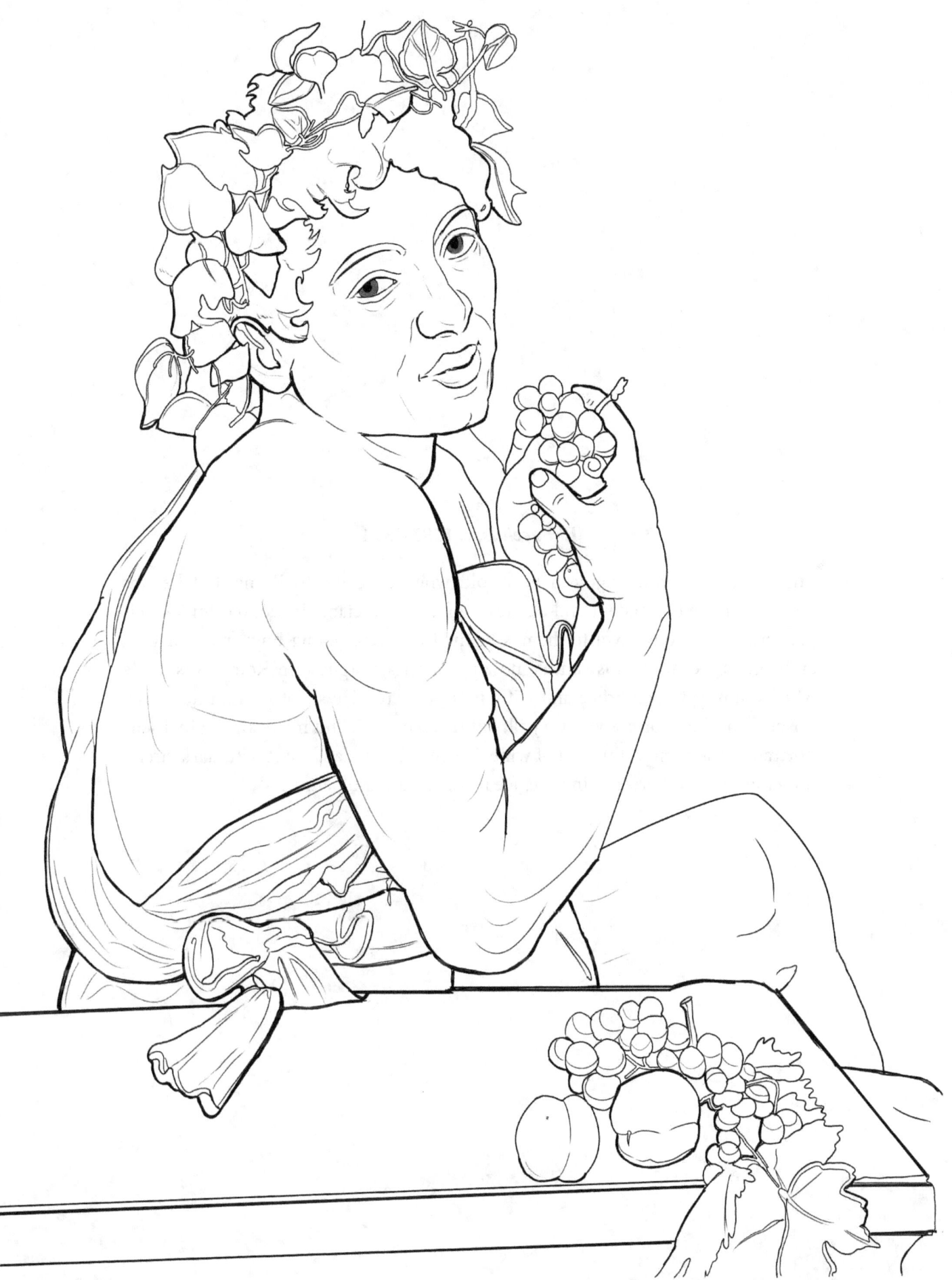

Plate 2.
Ill Bacchus, c. 1593-1594

The painter was only eighteen years old when he came to Rome, but he was enthusiastic, self-confident and already a great technician. He worked for various patrons, and among favorite themes of his time were young boys, painted with ambiguous meaning. This canvas, now in Galleria Borghese in Rome, was made when Caravaggio was broke and without a protector. He spent six months in the hospital for the poor. He was very ill, but he recovered, and made an original self-portrait. Caravaggio is this god of wine, joy, music and dance, but with dark circles under his eyes and green skin tone. He is weak, pale and penniless.

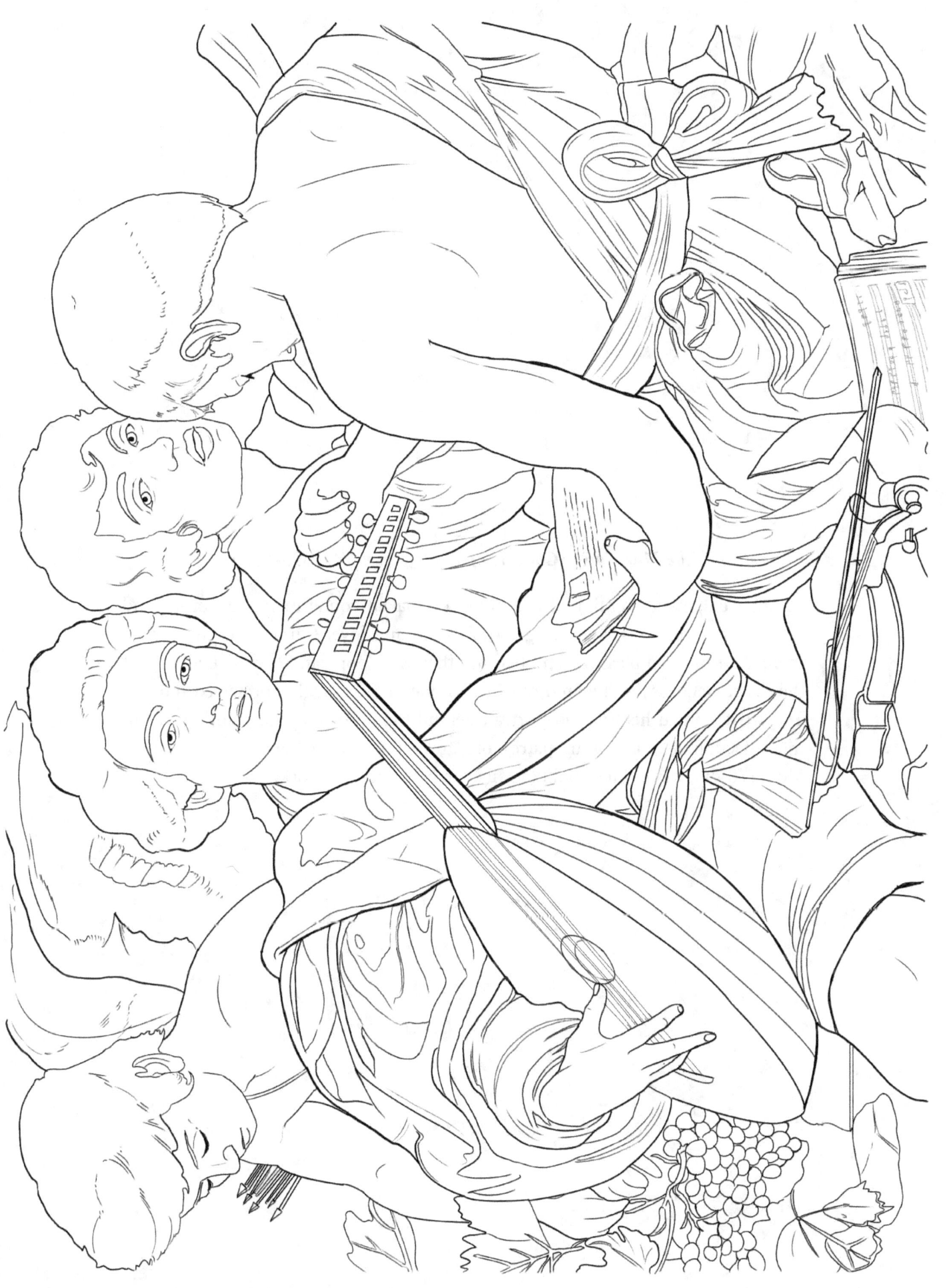

Plate 3.
The Musicians, (Concert of Young People) **c. 1595-1596**

Another enigmatic painting of beautiful, half naked young men, with erotic and sexual sensation. This is an allegory of music and love. Caravaggio chose such themes for his own pleasure, and because they were popular. Scholars believe that the instrument player, the amorous boy, is one of Caravaggio's preferred models. The artist painted his first self-portrait behind the musician. The painting was in the collection of an important patron of Caravaggio-Cardinal Francesco Maria del Monte. Today, it is in Metropolitan Museum of Art in New York.

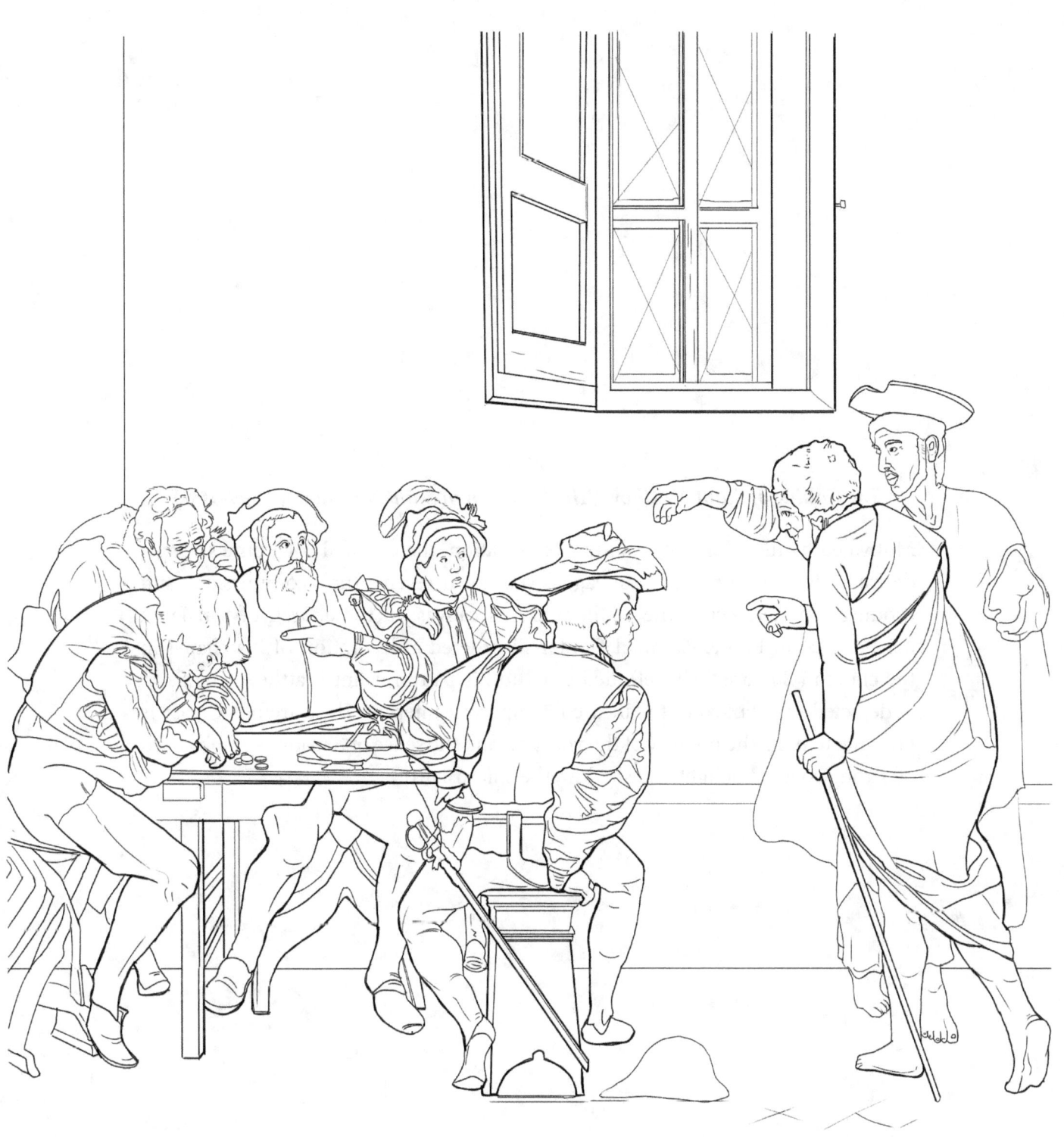

Plate 4.
The Calling of Saint Matthew (The Vocation of Saint Matthew), 1599-1600

Motivated by the efforts of Counter-Reformation, the cardinals of Rome strongly desired religious paintings. Caravaggio started to receive such commissions and produced masterpieces. One of them is this canvas, in the church of San Luigi dei Francesi in Rome. Cardinal Contarelli ordered a decoration of his chapel in the church (Contarelli chapel), dedicated to his patron, Saint Matthew. The Saint is depicted as a tax-collector in a contemporary interior. The barefoot Christ is pointing to him. The mystery of the vocation and the sense of tension is emphasized by strong contrast of light and shadow, the chiaroscuro.

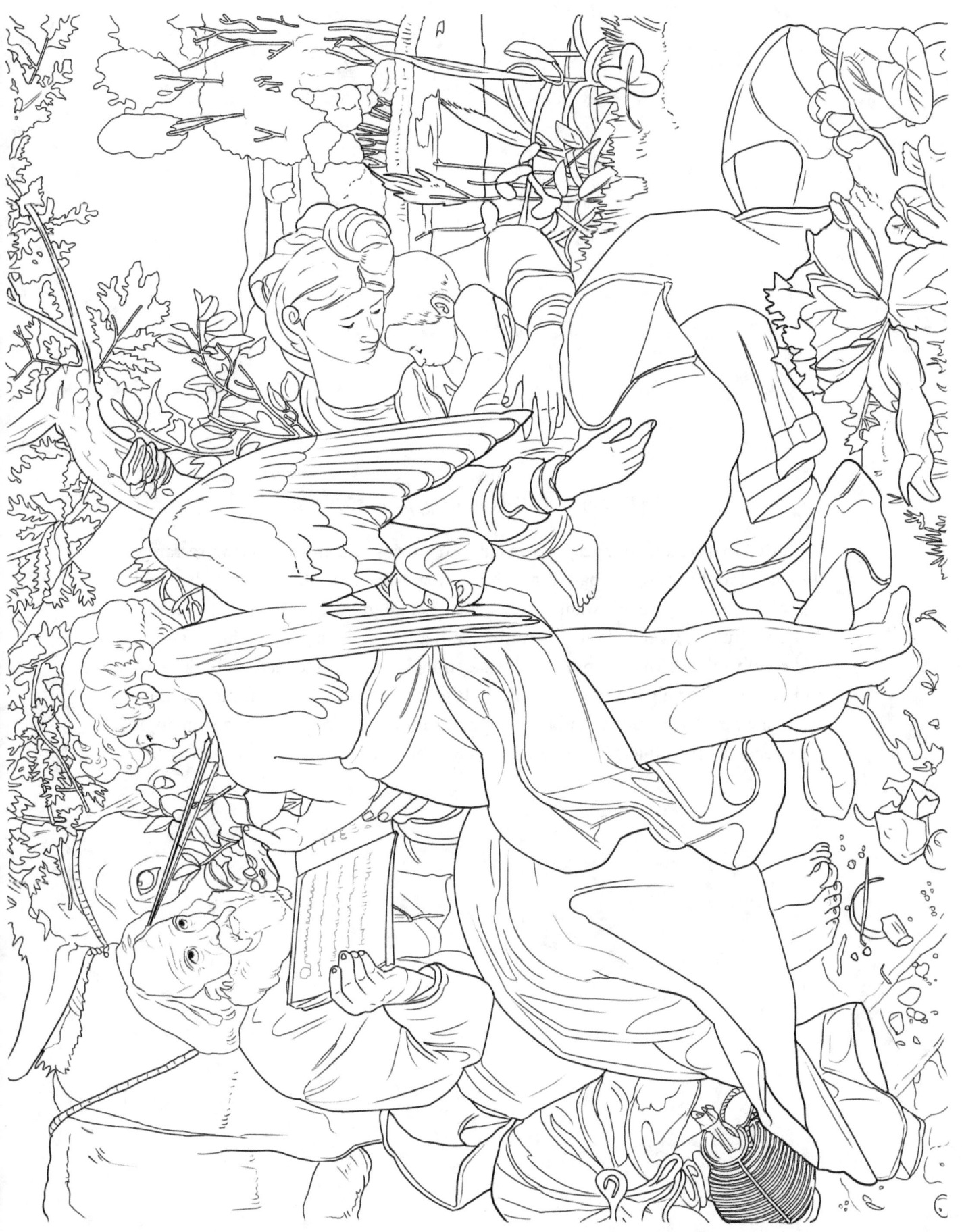

11

Plate 5.
The Rest on the Flight into Egypt, c. 1596-159

Caravaggio selected strange parts of Biblical stories and motifs that were rarely Illustrated for his religious paintings. The viewers were shocked, and they disputed his work. Ordinary people wanted to see idealized, dignified martyrs, not peasants and prostitutes. His holy family is resting, and an angel is playing violin to amuse and comfort them. The composition is exceptional. The angel turned his back to us, and he is almost vulgar and lascivious. St. Joseph is depicted as a common farmer, astonished by divine music, and the sleeping Virgin was recognized as a woman of the street. The painting is in Galleria Doria Pamphilj in Rome.

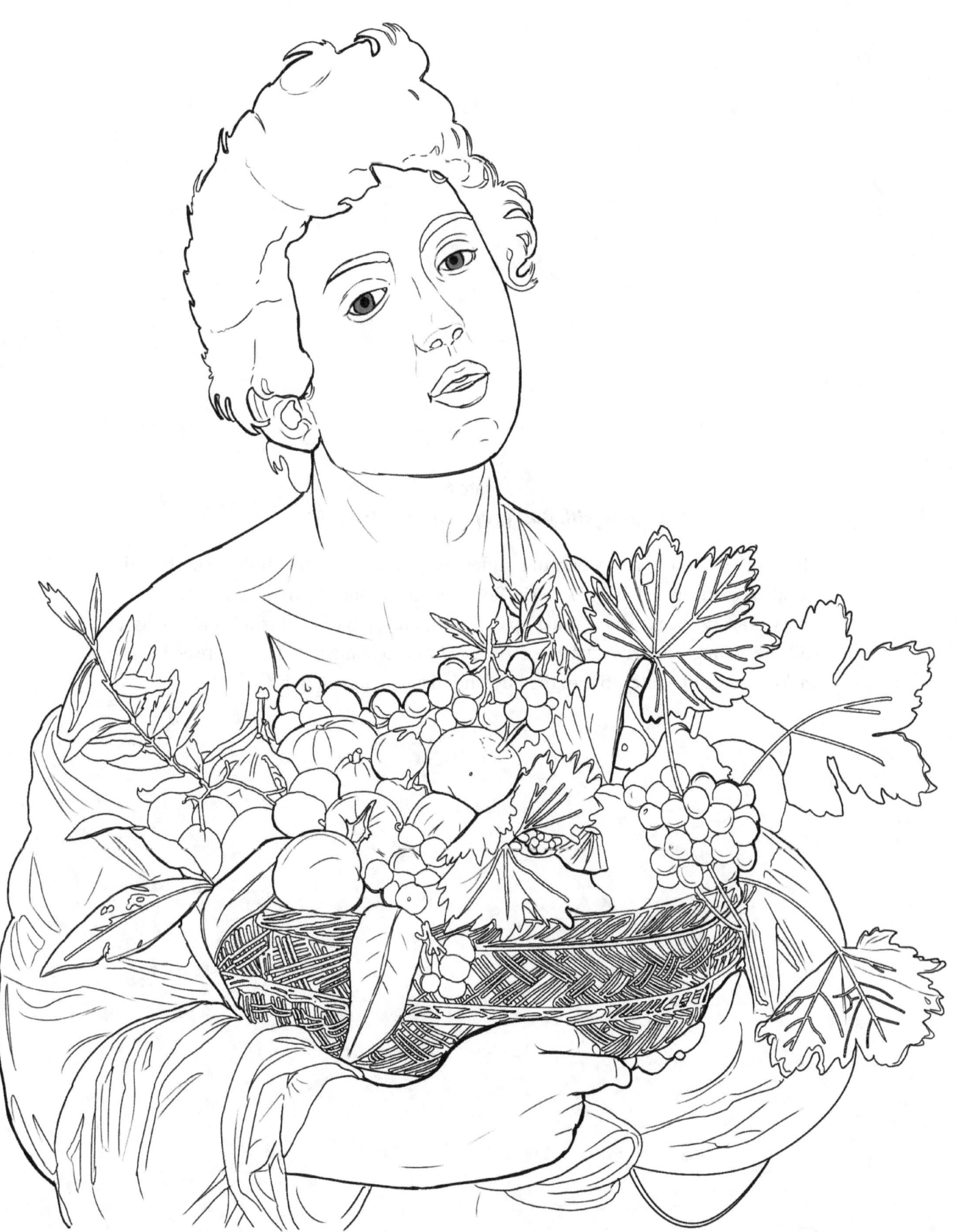

Plate 6.
Boy with Basket of Fruit, c. 1593-1594

This is one of Caravaggio's works done after his long illness, in the studio of his friend, Cavaliere d'Arpino. It is in Galleria Borghese in Rome. He depicted a charming boy, with rosy cheeks and sensual lips. He is holding a basket of fruits, painted as a still-life, with great virtuosity. The artist used his acclaimed contrast, between dark background and white attire of the boy, and diagonal line of light.

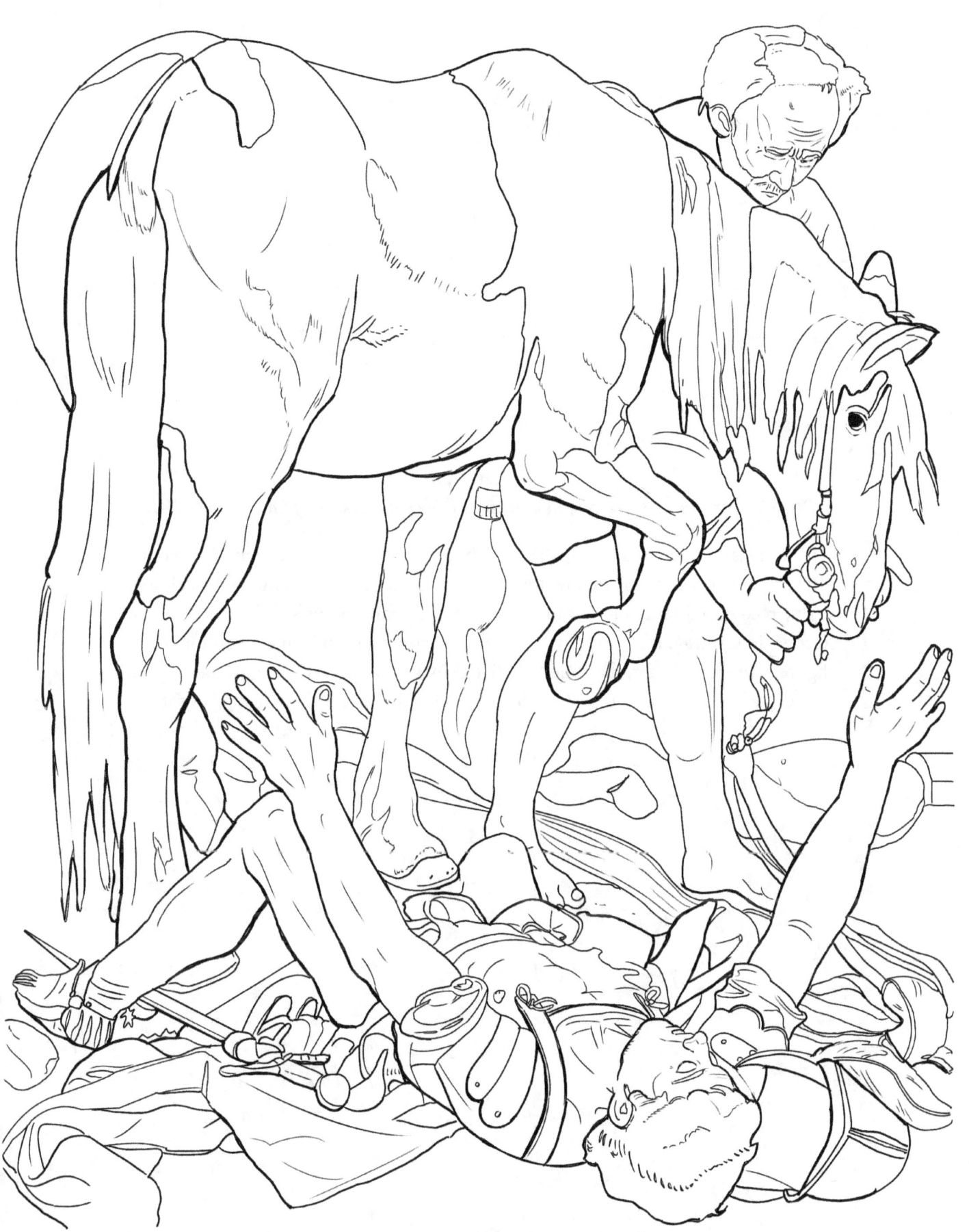

15

Plate 7.
The Conversion on the Way to Damascus (The Conversion of Saint Paul) **1601**

This canvas is in the Cerasi Chapel, in the church of Santa Maria del Popolo in Rome. The artist represented the moment when St. Paul fell of a horse, blinded by celestial light, recognized God and became Cristian. The painting was done for Cardinal Cerasi, in Caravaggio's distinctive manner: the composition is unconventional, the figures are radically foreshortened, depicted in a shallow space. He used energetic gestures, diagonal line of light and chiaroscuro to dramatize this spiritual event.

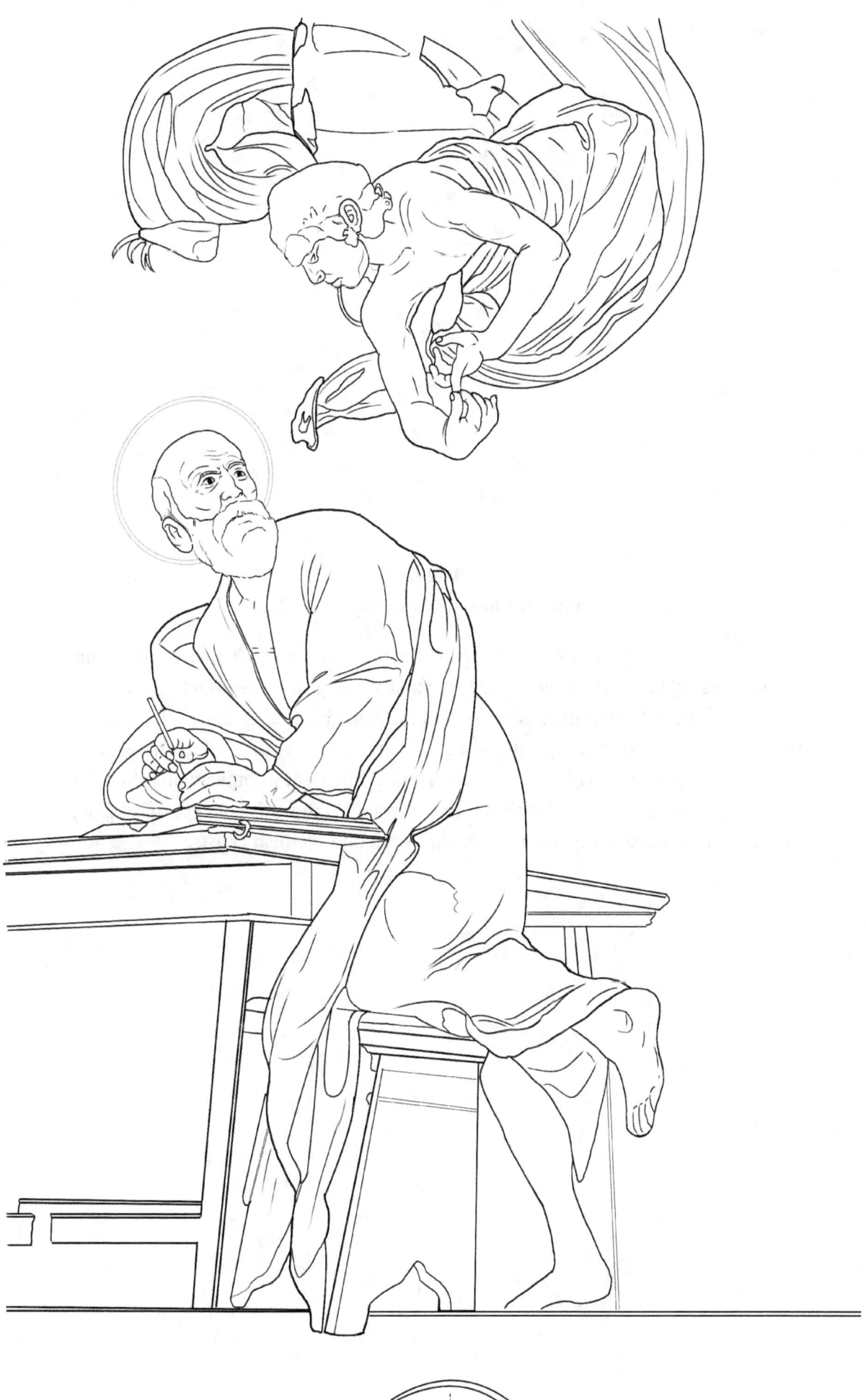

Plate 8.
Saint Matthew and the Angel, **1602**

This painting was done for the altarpiece of the Contarelli Chapel of San Luigi dei Francesi church in Rome. Today it stands alongside *The Martyrdom of St. Matthew* and *The Calling of St. Matthew,* as the artist himself arranged them. Here, an acrobatic angel encourages the saint to write. The revealing of great religious secrets is spontaneous, with lots of passion and excitement in movements. Nothing about faith is complicated or abstract for Caravaggio, and this concept of religious paintings influenced many Italian, French, Dutch and Flemish artists.